Other Books By Diana Rowe

Born to Die in My Place: A Timeless Story-Book 1
Born to Die in My Place: A Story of Unconditional Love-Book 2
An Invitation to the Sanctuary
How to Step Out of Grief and Bloom: A Practical Guide

Copyright 2020
Lillie of the Vallie, LLC
United States of America

Print ISBN: 978-1-7326972-6-3

Credits to the Holy Bible

Dedication

This journal is dedicated to People who want to step out of grief and bloom, with the power of God. This journal is an effective tool to help anyone who is grieving the loss of a loved one who passed away, experienced a divorce, a crushed friendship, family abandonment, or other significant losses.
You are not alone or forgotten.

Father in Heaven,
As I embark upon this journey to overcome grief, I am asking you to grant me wisdom, knowledge, understanding, and strength. Help me to keep my hand and my heart close to you. Please take charge of all the feelings inside my body, mind, and soul; and heal me in the mighty name of Jesus.
Amen

Theme of Content

Beginning with Self-Care.....2

Forgiveness Gratitude Victories

Window of Inspiration.....52

Letter Writing Care.....68

Honor the Memory.....70

Positive People List.....72

Laughter.....74

Holiday/Special Days Plan.....78

Letter to Self.....84, 86

Positive Self Reflection.....85

Letter to Family/Friend.....88

Letter to Jesus.....90

Spiritual Care.....92

Helping Others.....96

Progress.....98

Congratulations & Goals.....102

Helpful Bible Texts.....

DATE:
TODAY'S TASKS

-
-
-
-
-
-
-
-
-
-

TODAY, GOD HAS GIVEN ME HIS SPIRIT OF POWER, LOVE & SELF-CONTROL.
2 TIMOTHY 1:7
I CAN BLOOM!

Prayer: Lord, I need your strength to get through this day, in Jesus name; Amen.

My Self-Care checklist:

Prayer/Read Bible - Breakfast - Shower - Hair - Dress - Exercise - Lunch - Prayer - Encourage 2 Persons - Local Support Groups - Dinner - Get my at home massage - Take a soothing bath - Get a cup of herbal tea. Take a nap. Eat lots of fruits & veggies. Hey! it's O.K. to smile, laugh or cry. Jesus loves me; it's time to love me too. Listen to calm classical music, nature sounds, Christian music. Start a garden or get a plant. Adopt a pet. It' alright if I Seek professional help/speak to a trained pastoral counselor at a local church. Who can I help today?

Right Now I Feel:

What Self-Care can help now?

I can forgive myself and:

I am Grateful for:

List Today's Victories:

DATE:

How did I bloom today? _____
_____
_____

How can I improve? _____
_____
_____

What did I learn so far? _____
_____
_____
_____
_____
_____
_____
_____
_____
_____

My Plans for tomorrow with God's help:
_____
_____
_____
_____
_____

Living to Serve:

Who can I help today/tomorrow? Volunteer at:
Soup kitchen   Nursing home   School   Church
Start a group that: Cooks   Sew   Make crafts to share
Collect: food   clothing   books for those in need.
Join a rescue organization to help people or animals
Share Bible studies   Share your journey...

DATE:
TODAY'S TASKS

-
-
-
-
-
-
-
-
-
-

GIVE ALL YOUR WORRIES TO JESUS, BECAUSE HE CARES FOR YOU. 1 PETER 5:7
I CAN BLOOM!

Prayer: Lord, I need your strength to get through this day, in Jesus name; Amen.

My Self-Care checklist :

Prayer/Read Bible - Breakfast - Shower - Hair - Dress - Exercise - Lunch - Prayer - Encourage 2 Persons - Local Support Groups - Dinner - Get my at home massage - Take a soothing bath - Get a cup of herbal tea. Take a nap. Eat lots of fruits & veggies. Hey! it's O.K. to smile, laugh or cry. Jesus loves me; it's time to love me too. Listen to calm classical music, nature sounds, Christian music. Start a garden or get a plant. Adopt a pet. It' alright if I Seek professional help/speak to a trained pastoral counselor at a local church. Who can I help today?

Right Now I Feel:
_____
_____

What Self-Care can help now?
_____
_____

I can forgive myself and:
_____
_____

I am Grateful for:
_____
_____
_____

List Today's Victories:
_____
_____
_____

DATE:

How did I bloom today?

_____
_____

How can I improve?

_____
_____

What did I learn so far?
_____
_____
_____
_____
_____
_____
_____
_____
_____

My Plans for tomorrow with God's help:
_____
_____
_____
_____

Living to Serve:

Who can I help today/tomorrow? Volunteer at:
Soup kitchen   Nursing home   School   Church
Start a group that: Cooks   Sew   Make crafts to share
Collect: food   clothing   books for those in need.
Join a rescue organization to help people or animals
Share Bible studies   Share your journey…

DATE:
TODAY'S TASKS
-
-
-
-
-
-
-
-
-
-

THE LORD YOUR GOD WILL GO WITH YOU. HE WILL NOT LEAVE YOU OR FORGET YOU. DEUT. 31:6
I CAN BLOOM!

Prayer: Lord, I need your strength to get through this day, in Jesus name; Amen.

My Self-Care checklist:

Prayer/Read Bible - Breakfast - Shower - Hair - Dress - Exercise - Lunch - Prayer - Encourage 2 Persons - Local Support Groups - Dinner - Get my at home massage - Take a soothing bath - Get a cup of herbal tea. Take a nap. Eat lots of fruits & veggies. Hey! it's O.K. to smile, laugh or cry. Jesus loves me; it's time to love me too. Listen to calm classical music, nature sounds, Christian music. Start a garden or get a plant. Adopt a pet. It' alright if I Seek professional help/speak to a trained pastoral counselor at a local church. Who can I help today?

Right Now I Feel:
_____
_____

What Self-Care can help now?
_____
_____

I can forgive myself and:
_____
_____

I am Grateful for:
_____
_____
_____

List Today's Victories:
_____
_____
_____

DATE: _____

How did I bloom today? _____
_____

How can I improve? _____
_____

What did I learn so far? _____
_____
_____
_____
_____
_____
_____
_____

My Plans for tomorrow with God's help: ____
_____
_____
_____
_____

Living to Serve:

Who can I help today/tomorrow? Volunteer at:
Soup kitchen   Nursing home   School   Church
Start a group that: Cooks   Sew   Make crafts to share
Collect: food   clothing   books for those in need.
Join a rescue organization to help people or animals
Share Bible studies   Share your journey…

DATE:
TODAY'S TASKS

-
-
-
-
-
-
-
-
-

THE LORD IS THE ONE WHO GOES AHEAD OF YOU; HE WILL BE WITH YOU. HE WILL NOT FAIL YOU OR FORSAKE YOU. DO NOT FEAR OR BE DISMAYED. DEUT. 31:8
I CAN BLOOM!

Prayer: Lord, I need your strength to get through this day, in Jesus name; Amen.

My Self-Care checklist:

Prayer/Read Bible - Breakfast - Shower - Hair - Dress - Exercise - Lunch - Prayer - Encourage 2 Persons - Local Support Groups - Dinner - Get my at home massage - Take a soothing bath - Get a cup of herbal tea. Take a nap. Eat lots of fruits & veggies. Hey! it's O.K. to smile, laugh or cry. Jesus loves me; it's time to love me too. Listen to calm classical music, nature sounds, Christian music. Start a garden or get a plant. Adopt a pet. It' alright if I Seek professional help/speak to a trained pastoral counselor at a local church. Who can I help today?

Right Now I Feel:
___
___

What Self-Care can help now?
___
___

I can forgive myself and:
___
___

I am Grateful for:
___
___
___

List Today's Victories:
___
___
___

DATE:

How did I bloom today?

How can I improve?

What did I learn so far?

My Plans for tomorrow with God's help:

Living to Serve:

Who can I help today/tomorrow? Volunteer at:
Soup kitchen   Nursing home   School   Church
Start a group that: Cooks   Sew   Make crafts to share
Collect: food   clothing   books for those in need.
Join a rescue organization to help people or animals
Share Bible studies   Share your journey...

DATE:
TODAY'S TASKS
-
-
-
-
-
-
-
-
-
-

WE CAN SAY WITH CONFIDENCE, "THE LORD IS MY HELPER; I WILL NOT BE AFRAID. WHAT CAN ANYONE DO TO ME?" HEBREWS 13:6
I CAN BLOOM!

Prayer: Lord, I need your strength to get through this day, in Jesus name; Amen.

My Self-Care checklist:

Prayer/Read Bible - Breakfast - Shower - Hair - Dress - Exercise - Lunch - Prayer - Encourage 2 Persons - Local Support Groups - Dinner - Get my at home massage - Take a soothing bath - Get a cup of herbal tea. Take a nap. Eat lots of fruits & veggies. Hey! it's O.K. to smile, laugh or cry. Jesus loves me; it's time to love me too. Listen to calm classical music, nature sounds, Christian music. Start a garden or get a plant. Adopt a pet. It' alright if I Seek professional help/speak to a trained pastoral counselor at a local church. Who can I help today?

Right Now I Feel: _____
_____
_____

What Self-Care can help now? _____
_____
_____

I can forgive myself and: _____
_____

I am Grateful for: _____
_____
_____

List Today's Victories: _____
_____
_____
_____

DATE:

How did I bloom today? _____

How can I improve? _____

What did I learn so far? _____
_____
_____
_____
_____
_____
_____
_____

My Plans for tomorrow with God's help: _____
_____
_____
_____

Living to Serve:

Who can I help today/tomorrow? Volunteer at:
Soup kitchen   Nursing home   School   Church
Start a group that: Cooks   Sew   Make crafts to share
Collect: food   clothing   books for those in need.
Join a rescue organization to help people or animals
Share Bible studies   Share your journey…

DATE:
TODAY'S TASKS

-
-
-
-
-
-
-
-
-

HE GIVES STRENGTH TO THE WEARY AND INCREASES THE POWER OF THE WEAK. ISAIAH 40:29
I CAN BLOOM!

Prayer: Lord, I need your strength to get through this day, in Jesus name; Amen.

My Self-Care checklist:

Prayer/Read Bible - Breakfast - Shower - Hair - Dress - Exercise - Lunch - Prayer - Encourage 2 Persons - Local Support Groups - Dinner - Get my at home massage - Take a soothing bath - Get a cup of herbal tea. Take a nap. Eat lots of fruits & veggies. Hey! it's O.K. to smile, laugh or cry. Jesus loves me; it's time to love me too. Listen to calm classical music, nature sounds, Christian music. Start a garden or get a plant. Adopt a pet. It' alright if I Seek professional help/speak to a trained pastoral counselor at a local church. Who can I help today?

Right Now I Feel:
___
___

What Self-Care can help now?
___
___

I can forgive myself and:
___
___

I am Grateful for:
___
___
___

List Today's Victories:
___
___
___

DATE: _____

How did I bloom today? _____
_____
_____

How can I improve? _____
_____

What did I learn so far?
_____
_____
_____
_____
_____
_____
_____
_____
_____

My Plans for tomorrow with God's help: _____
_____
_____
_____
_____

Living to Serve:

Who can I help today/tomorrow? Volunteer at:
Soup kitchen   Nursing home   School   Church
Start a group that: Cooks   Sew   Make crafts to share
Collect: food   clothing   books for those in need.
Join a rescue organization to help people or animals
Share Bible studies   Share your journey…

DATE:
TODAY'S TASKS
-
-
-
-
-
-
-
-
-

DO NOT FEAR, FOR I AM WITH YOU; DO NOT ANXIOUSLY LOOK ABOUT YOU, FOR I AM YOUR GOD. I WILL STRENGTHEN YOU, SURELY I WILL HELP YOU, SURELY I WILL UPHOLD YOU WITH MY RIGHTEOUS RIGHT HAND. ISAIAH 41:10
I CAN BLOOM!

Prayer: Lord, I need your strength to get through this day, in Jesus name; Amen.

My Self-Care checklist:

Prayer/Read Bible - Breakfast - Shower - Hair - Dress - Exercise - Lunch - Prayer - Encourage 2 Persons - Local Support Groups - Dinner - Get my at home massage - Take a soothing bath - Get a cup of herbal tea. Take a nap. Eat lots of fruits & veggies. Hey! it's O.K. to smile, laugh or cry. Jesus loves me; it's time to love me too. Listen to calm classical music, nature sounds, Christian music. Start a garden or get a plant. Adopt a pet. It' alright if I Seek professional help/speak to a trained pastoral counselor at a local church. Who can I help today?

Right Now I Feel: _____
_____
_____

What Self-Care can help now? _____
_____
_____

I can forgive myself and: _____
_____
_____

I am Grateful for: _____
_____
_____

List Today's Victories: _____
_____
_____
_____

DATE: _____

How did I bloom today? _____
_____

How can I improve? _____
_____

What did I learn so far?
_____
_____
_____
_____
_____
_____

My Plans for tomorrow with God's help:
_____
_____
_____
_____
_____

Living to Serve:

Who can I help today/tomorrow? Volunteer at:
Soup kitchen   Nursing home   School   Church
Start a group that: Cooks   Sew   Make crafts to share
Collect: food   clothing   books for those in need.
Join a rescue organization to help people or animals
Share Bible studies   Share your journey...

DATE:
TODAY'S TASKS
-
-
-
-
-
-
-
-
-
-

FOR THE MOUNTAINS MAY DEPART AND THE HILLS BE REMOVED, BUT MY STEADFAST LOVE SHALL NOT DEPART FROM YOU. ISAIAH 54:10
I CAN BLOOM!

Prayer: Lord, I need your strength to get through this day, in Jesus name; Amen.

My Self-Care checklist:

Prayer/Read Bible - Breakfast - Shower - Hair - Dress - Exercise - Lunch - Prayer - Encourage 2 Persons - Local Support Groups - Dinner - Get my at home massage - Take a soothing bath - Get a cup of herbal tea. Take a nap. Eat lots of fruits & veggies. Hey! it's O.K. to smile, laugh or cry. Jesus loves me; it's time to love me too. Listen to calm classical music, nature sounds, Christian music. Start a garden or get a plant. Adopt a pet. It' alright if I Seek professional help/speak to a trained pastoral counselor at a local church. Who can I help today?

Right Now I Feel:
_____
_____

What Self-Care can help now?
_____
_____

I can forgive myself and:
_____
_____

I am Grateful for:
_____
_____
_____

List Today's Victories:
_____
_____
_____

DATE:

How did I bloom today?

How can I improve?

What did I learn so far?

My Plans for tomorrow with God's help:

Living to Serve:

Who can I help today/tomorrow? Volunteer at:
Soup kitchen   Nursing home   School   Church
Start a group that: Cooks   Sew   Make crafts to share
Collect: food   clothing   books for those in need.
Join a rescue organization to help people or animals
Share Bible studies   Share your journey...

DATE:
TODAY'S TASKS
-
-
-
-
-
-
-
-
-

I HAVE LOVED YOU WITH AN EVERLASTING LOVE; I HAVE DRAWN YOU WITH UNFAILING KINDNESS.
JEREMIAH 31:3
I CAN BLOOM!

Prayer: Lord, I need your strength to get through this day, in Jesus name; Amen.

My Self-Care checklist:

Prayer/Read Bible - Breakfast - Shower - Hair - Dress - Exercise - Lunch - Prayer - Encourage 2 Persons - Local Support Groups - Dinner - Get my at home massage - Take a soothing bath - Get a cup of herbal tea. Take a nap. Eat lots of fruits & veggies. Hey! it's O.K. to smile, laugh or cry. Jesus loves me; it's time to love me too. Listen to calm classical music, nature sounds, Christian music. Start a garden or get a plant. Adopt a pet. It' alright if I Seek professional help/speak to a trained pastoral counselor at a local church. Who can I help today?

Right Now I Feel:
_____
_____
_____

What Self-Care can help now?
_____
_____

I can forgive myself and:
_____
_____

I am Grateful for:
_____
_____
_____

List Today's Victories:
_____
_____
_____

DATE:

How did I bloom today? _____

How can I improve? _____

What did I learn so far?
_____
_____
_____
_____
_____
_____
_____

My Plans for tomorrow with God's help:
_____
_____
_____
_____
_____

Living to Serve:

Who can I help today/tomorrow? Volunteer at:
Soup kitchen   Nursing home   School   Church
Start a group that: Cooks   Sew   Make crafts to share
Collect: food   clothing   books for those in need.
Join a rescue organization to help people or animals
Share Bible studies   Share your journey…

DATE:
TODAY'S TASKS

-
-
-
-
-
-
-
-
-

GOD HAS SENT ME [JESUS] TO HEAL THE BROKENHEARTED.
LUKE 4:18
I CAN BLOOM!

Prayer: Lord, I need your strength to get through this day, in Jesus name; Amen.

My Self-Care checklist :

Prayer/Read Bible - Breakfast - Shower - Hair - Dress - Exercise - Lunch - Prayer - Encourage 2 Persons - Local Support Groups - Dinner - Get my at home massage - Take a soothing bath - Get a cup of herbal tea. Take a nap. Eat lots of fruits & veggies. Hey! it's O.K. to smile, laugh or cry. Jesus loves me; it's time to love me too. Listen to calm classical music, nature sounds, Christian music. Start a garden or get a plant. Adopt a pet. It' alright if I Seek professional help/speak to a trained pastoral counselor at a local church. Who can I help today?

Right Now I Feel:

What Self-Care can help now?

I can forgive myself and:

I am Grateful for:

List Today's Victories:

DATE: _____

How did I bloom today?

How can I improve?

What did I learn so far?
_____
_____
_____
_____
_____
_____
_____

My Plans for tomorrow with God's help:
_____
_____
_____
_____
_____

Living to Serve:

Who can I help today/tomorrow? Volunteer at:
Soup kitchen   Nursing home   School   Church
Start a group that: Cooks   Sew   Make crafts to share
Collect: food   clothing   books for those in need.
Join a rescue organization to help people or animals
Share Bible studies   Share your journey...

DATE:
TODAY'S TASKS

-
-
-
-
-
-
-
-
-
-

BLESSED ARE THOSE WHO MOURN, FOR THEY SHALL BE COMFORTED.
MATTHEW 5:4
I CAN BLOOM!

Prayer: Lord, I need your strength to get through this day, in Jesus name; Amen.

My Self-Care checklist:

Prayer/Read Bible - Breakfast - Shower - Hair - Dress - Exercise - Lunch - Prayer - Encourage 2 Persons - Local Support Groups - Dinner - Get my at home massage - Take a soothing bath - Get a cup of herbal tea. Take a nap. Eat lots of fruits & veggies. Hey! it's O.K. to smile, laugh or cry. Jesus loves me; it's time to love me too. Listen to calm classical music, nature sounds, Christian music. Start a garden or get a plant. Adopt a pet. It' alright if I Seek professional help/speak to a trained pastoral counselor at a local church. Who can I help today?

Right Now I Feel:

What Self-Care can help now?

I can forgive myself and:

I am Grateful for:

List Today's Victories:

DATE: _____

How did I bloom today? _____
_____
_____

How can I improve? _____
_____
_____

What did I learn so far? _____
_____
_____
_____
_____
_____
_____
_____

My Plans for tomorrow with God's help:
_____
_____
_____
_____
_____

Living to Serve:

Who can I help today/tomorrow? Volunteer at:
Soup kitchen   Nursing home   School   Church
Start a group that: Cooks   Sew   Make crafts to share
Collect: food   clothing   books for those in need.
Join a rescue organization to help people or animals
Share Bible studies   Share your journey...

DATE:
TODAY'S TASKS
-
-
-
-
-
-
-
-
-

DO NOT SORROW, FOR THE JOY OF THE LORD IS YOUR STRENGTH.
NEHEMIAH 8:10
I CAN BLOOM!

Prayer: Lord, I need your strength to get through this day, in Jesus name; Amen.

My Self-Care checklist :

Prayer/Read Bible - Breakfast - Shower - Hair - Dress - Exercise - Lunch- Prayer - Encourage 2 Persons - Local Support Groups - Dinner - Get my at home massage - Take a soothing bath - Get a cup of herbal tea. Take a nap. Eat lots of fruits & veggies. Hey! it's O.K. to smile, laugh or cry. Jesus loves me; it's time to love me too. Listen to calm classical music, nature sounds, Christian music. Start a garden or get a plant. Adopt a pet. It' alright if I Seek professional help/speak to a trained pastoral counselor at a local church. Who can I help today?

Right Now I Feel:
_____
_____

What Self-Care can help now?
_____
_____

I can forgive myself and:
_____
_____

I am Grateful for:
_____
_____
_____

List Today's Victories:
_____
_____
_____

DATE:

How did I bloom today?

_____
_____

How can I improve?

_____
_____

What did I learn so far?
_____
_____
_____
_____
_____
_____
_____
_____

My Plans for tomorrow with God's help:
_____
_____
_____
_____
_____
_____

Living to Serve:

Who can I help today/tomorrow? Volunteer at:
Soup kitchen   Nursing home   School   Church
Start a group that: Cooks   Sew   Make crafts to share
Collect: food   clothing   books for those in need.
Join a rescue organization to help people or animals
Share Bible studies   Share your journey...

DATE:
TODAY'S TASKS
-
-
-
-
-
-
-
-
-

I LOVE THE LORD, BECAUSE HE HEARS MY VOICE AND MY SUPPLICATIONS.
PSALM 116:1
I CAN BLOOM!

Prayer: Lord, I need your strength to get through this day, in Jesus name; Amen.

My Self-Care checklist:

Prayer/Read Bible - Breakfast - Shower - Hair - Dress - Exercise - Lunch - Prayer - Encourage 2 Persons - Local Support Groups - Dinner - Get my at home massage - Take a soothing bath - Get a cup of herbal tea. Take a nap. Eat lots of fruits & veggies. Hey! it's O.K. to smile, laugh or cry. Jesus loves me; it's time to love me too. Listen to calm classical music, nature sounds, Christian music. Start a garden or get a plant. Adopt a pet. It' alright if I Seek professional help/speak to a trained pastoral counselor at a local church. Who can I help today?

Right Now I Feel:
_____
_____

What Self-Care can help now?
_____
_____

I can forgive myself and:
_____
_____

I am Grateful for:
_____
_____
_____

List Today's Victories:
_____
_____
_____
_____

DATE:

How did I bloom today?

How can I improve?

What did I learn so far?

My Plans for tomorrow with God's help:

Living to Serve:

Who can I help today/tomorrow? Volunteer at:
Soup kitchen   Nursing home   School   Church
Start a group that: Cooks   Sew   Make crafts to share
Collect: food   clothing   books for those in need.
Join a rescue organization to help people or animals
Share Bible studies   Share your journey...

DATE:
TODAY'S TASKS
-
-
-
-
-
-
-
-
-

THIS IS MY COMFORT IN MY AFFLICTION, THAT YOUR WORD HAS REVIVED ME. PSALM 119:50
I CAN BLOOM!

Prayer: Lord, I need your strength to get through this day, in Jesus name; Amen.

My Self-Care checklist :

Prayer/Read Bible - Breakfast - Shower - Hair - Dress - Exercise - Lunch - Prayer - Encourage 2 Persons - Local Support Groups - Dinner - Get my at home massage - Take a soothing bath - Get a cup of herbal tea. Take a nap. Eat lots of fruits & veggies. Hey! it's O.K. to smile, laugh or cry. Jesus loves me; it's time to love me too. Listen to calm classical music, nature sounds, Christian music. Start a garden or get a plant. Adopt a pet. It' alright if I Seek professional help/speak to a trained pastoral counselor at a local church. Who can I help today?

Right Now I Feel:

What Self-Care can help now?

I can forgive myself and:

I am Grateful for:

List Today's Victories:

DATE: _____

How did I bloom today?
_____
_____

How can I improve?
_____
_____

What did I learn so far?
_____
_____
_____
_____
_____
_____
_____
_____

My Plans for tomorrow with God's help:
_____
_____
_____
_____
_____

Living to Serve:

Who can I help today/tomorrow? Volunteer at:
Soup kitchen   Nursing home   School   Church
Start a group that: Cooks   Sew   Make crafts to share
Collect: food   clothing   books for those in need.
Join a rescue organization to help people or animals
Share Bible studies   Share your journey...

DATE:
TODAY'S TASKS
-
-
-
-
-
-
-
-
-
-

THE LORD IS GRACIOUS AND FULL OF COMPASSION.
PSALM 145:8
I CAN BLOOM!

Prayer: Lord, I need your strength to get through this day, in Jesus name; Amen.

My Self-Care checklist:

Prayer/Read Bible - Breakfast - Shower - Hair - Dress - Exercise - Lunch - Prayer - Encourage 2 Persons - Local Support Groups - Dinner - Get my at home massage - Take a soothing bath - Get a cup of herbal tea. Take a nap. Eat lots of fruits & veggies. Hey! it's O.K. to smile, laugh or cry. Jesus loves me; it's time to love me too. Listen to calm classical music, nature sounds, Christian music. Start a garden or get a plant. Adopt a pet. It' alright if I Seek professional help/speak to a trained pastoral counselor at a local church. Who can I help today?

Right Now I Feel:

What Self-Care can help now?

I can forgive myself and:

I am Grateful for:

List Today's Victories:

DATE:

How did I bloom today?

How can I improve?

What did I learn so far?

My Plans for tomorrow with God's help:

Living to Serve:

Who can I help today/tomorrow? Volunteer at:
Soup kitchen   Nursing home   School   Church
Start a group that: Cooks   Sew   Make crafts to share
Collect: food   clothing   books for those in need.
Join a rescue organization to help people or animals
Share Bible studies   Share your journey...

DATE:
TODAY'S TASKS

-
-
-
-
-
-
-
-
-

HE HEALS THE BROKENHEARTED. HE BANDAGES THEIR WOUNDS.
PSALM 147:3
I CAN BLOOM!

Prayer: Lord, I need your strength to get through this day, in Jesus name; Amen.

My Self-Care checklist :

Prayer/Read Bible - Breakfast - Shower - Hair - Dress - Exercise - Lunch - Prayer - Encourage 2 Persons - Local Support Groups - Dinner - Get my at home massage - Take a soothing bath - Get a cup of herbal tea. Take a nap. Eat lots of fruits & veggies. Hey! it's O.K. to smile, laugh or cry. Jesus loves me; it's time to love me too. Listen to calm classical music, nature sounds, Christian music. Start a garden or get a plant. Adopt a pet. It' alright if I Seek professional help/speak to a trained pastoral counselor at a local church. Who can I help today?

Right Now I Feel:

What Self-Care can help now?

I can forgive myself and:

I am Grateful for:

List Today's Victories:

DATE:

How did I bloom today?

How can I improve?

What did I learn so far?

My Plans for tomorrow with God's help:

Living to Serve:

Who can I help today/tomorrow? Volunteer at:
Soup kitchen   Nursing home   School   Church
Start a group that: Cooks   Sew   Make crafts to share
Collect: food   clothing   books for those in need.
Join a rescue organization to help people or animals
Share Bible studies   Share your journey…

DATE:
TODAY'S TASKS
-
-
-
-
-
-
-
-
-

BUT THE SALVATION OF THE RIGHTEOUS IS FROM THE LORD; HE IS THEIR STRENGTH IN THE TIME OF TROUBLE. PSALM 37:39
I CAN BLOOM!

Prayer: Lord, I need your strength to get through this day, in Jesus name; Amen.

My Self-Care checklist:

Prayer/Read Bible - Breakfast - Shower - Hair - Dress - Exercise - Lunch - Prayer - Encourage 2 Persons - Local Support Groups - Dinner - Get my at home massage - Take a soothing bath - Get a cup of herbal tea. Take a nap. Eat lots of fruits & veggies. Hey! it's O.K. to smile, laugh or cry. Jesus loves me; it's time to love me too. Listen to calm classical music, nature sounds, Christian music. Start a garden or get a plant. Adopt a pet. It' alright if I Seek professional help/speak to a trained pastoral counselor at a local church. Who can I help today?

Right Now I Feel:

What Self-Care can help now?

I can forgive myself and:

I am Grateful for:

List Today's Victories:

DATE: _____

How did I bloom today? _____
_____
_____

How can I improve? _____
_____

What did I learn so far?
_____
_____
_____
_____
_____
_____
_____

My Plans for tomorrow with God's help:
_____
_____
_____
_____
_____

Living to Serve:

Who can I help today/tomorrow? Volunteer at:
Soup kitchen   Nursing home   School   Church
Start a group that: Cooks   Sew   Make crafts to share
Collect: food   clothing   books for those in need.
Join a rescue organization to help people or animals
Share Bible studies   Share your journey...

DATE:
TODAY'S TASKS
-
-
-
-
-
-
-
-
-

GOD IS OUR PROTECTION AND OUR STRENGTH. HE ALWAYS HELPS IN TIMES OF TROUBLE.
PSALM 46:1
I CAN BLOOM!

Prayer: Lord, I need your strength to get through this day, in Jesus name; Amen.

My Self-Care checklist:

Prayer/Read Bible - Breakfast - Shower - Hair - Dress - Exercise - Lunch- Prayer - Encourage 2 Persons - Local Support Groups - Dinner - Get my at home massage - Take a soothing bath - Get a cup of herbal tea. Take a nap. Eat lots of fruits & veggies. Hey! it's O.K. to smile, laugh or cry. Jesus loves me; it's time to love me too. Listen to calm classical music, nature sounds, Christian music. Start a garden or get a plant. Adopt a pet. It' alright if I Seek professional help/speak to a trained pastoral counselor at a local church. Who can I help today?

Right Now I Feel:

What Self-Care can help now?

I can forgive myself and:

I am Grateful for:

List Today's Victories:

DATE:

How did I bloom today?

How can I improve?

What did I learn so far?

My Plans for tomorrow with God's help:

Living to Serve:

Who can I help today/tomorrow? Volunteer at:
Soup kitchen   Nursing home   School   Church
Start a group that: Cooks   Sew   Make crafts to share
Collect: food   clothing   books for those in need.
Join a rescue organization to help people or animals
Share Bible studies   Share your journey...

DATE:
TODAY'S TASKS
-
-
-
-
-
-
-
-
-

YOU ARE MY
PROTECTION, MY
PLACE OF
SAFETY IN TIMES
OF TROUBLE.
PSALM 59:16
I CAN BLOOM!

Prayer: Lord, I need your strength to get through this day, in Jesus name; Amen.

My Self-Care checklist :

Prayer/Read Bible - Breakfast - Shower - Hair - Dress - Exercise - Lunch- Prayer - Encourage 2 Persons - Local Support Groups - Dinner - Get my at home massage - Take a soothing bath - Get a cup of herbal tea. Take a nap. Eat lots of fruits & veggies. Hey! it's O.K. to smile, laugh or cry. Jesus loves me; it's time to love me too. Listen to calm classical music, nature sounds, Christian music. Start a garden or get a plant. Adopt a pet. It' alright if I Seek professional help/speak to a trained pastoral counselor at a local church. Who can I help today?

Right Now I Feel: _____
_____
_____

What Self-Care can help now? _____
_____
_____

I can forgive myself and: _____
_____
_____

I am Grateful for: _____
_____
_____
_____

List Today's Victories: _____
_____
_____
_____
_____

DATE:

How did I bloom today?

How can I improve?

What did I learn so far?

My Plans for tomorrow with God's help:

Living to Serve:

Who can I help today/tomorrow? Volunteer at:
Soup kitchen   Nursing home   School   Church
Start a group that: Cooks   Sew   Make crafts to share
Collect: food   clothing   books for those in need.
Join a rescue organization to help people or animals
Share Bible studies   Share your journey…

DATE:
TODAY'S TASKS

-
-
-
-
-
-
-
-
-

MY SOUL, WAIT IN SILENCE FOR GOD ONLY, FOR MY HOPE IS FROM HIM.
PSALM 62:5
I CAN BLOOM!

Prayer: Lord, I need your strength to get through this day, in Jesus name; Amen.

My Self-Care checklist:

Prayer/Read Bible - Breakfast - Shower - Hair - Dress - Exercise - Lunch- Prayer - Encourage 2 Persons - Local Support Groups - Dinner - Get my at home massage - Take a soothing bath - Get a cup of herbal tea. Take a nap. Eat lots of fruits & veggies. Hey! it's O.K. to smile, laugh or cry. Jesus loves me; it's time to love me too. Listen to calm classical music, nature sounds, Christian music. Start a garden or get a plant. Adopt a pet. It' alright if I Seek professional help/speak to a trained pastoral counselor at a local church. Who can I help today?

Right Now I Feel:

What Self-Care can help now?

I can forgive myself and:

I am Grateful for:

List Today's Victories:

DATE:

How did I bloom today?

How can I improve?

What did I learn so far?

My Plans for tomorrow with God's help:

Living to Serve:

Who can I help today/tomorrow? Volunteer at:
Soup kitchen   Nursing home   School   Church
Start a group that: Cooks   Sew   Make crafts to share
Collect: food   clothing   books for those in need.
Join a rescue organization to help people or animals
Share Bible studies   Share your journey...

DATE:
TODAY'S TASKS
-
-
-
-
-
-
-
-
-

MY FLESH AND MY HEART FAIL; BUT GOD IS THE STRENGTH OF MY HEART AND MY PORTION FOREVER.
PSALM 73:26
I CAN BLOOM!

Prayer: Lord, I need your strength to get through this day, in Jesus name; Amen.

My Self-Care checklist:

Prayer/Read Bible - Breakfast - Shower - Hair - Dress - Exercise - Lunch - Prayer - Encourage 2 Persons - Local Support Groups - Dinner - Get my at home massage - Take a soothing bath - Get a cup of herbal tea. Take a nap. Eat lots of fruits & veggies. Hey! it's O.K. to smile, laugh or cry. Jesus loves me; it's time to love me too. Listen to calm classical music, nature sounds, Christian music. Start a garden or get a plant. Adopt a pet. It' alright if I Seek professional help/speak to a trained pastoral counselor at a local church. Who can I help today?

Right Now I Feel: _____

What Self-Care can help now? _____

I can forgive myself and: _____

I am Grateful for: _____

List Today's Victories: _____

How did I bloom today?

How can I improve?

What did I learn so far?

My Plans for tomorrow with God's help:

Living to Serve:

Who can I help today/tomorrow? Volunteer at:
Soup kitchen   Nursing home   School   Church
Start a group that: Cooks   Sew   Make crafts to share
Collect: food   clothing   books for those in need.
Join a rescue organization to help people or animals
Share Bible studies   Share your journey...

DATE:
TODAY'S TASKS

-
-
-
-
-
-
-
-
-
-

HE WILL WIPE AWAY EVERY TEAR FROM THEIR EYES. THERE WILL BE NO MORE DEATH, SADNESS, CRYING, OR PAIN. ALL THE OLD WAYS ARE GONE.
REVELATION 21:4
I CAN BLOOM!

Prayer: Lord, I need your strength to get through this day, in Jesus name; Amen.

My Self-Care checklist:

Prayer/Read Bible - Breakfast - Shower - Hair - Dress - Exercise - Lunch - Prayer - Encourage 2 Persons - Local Support Groups - Dinner - Get my at home massage - Take a soothing bath - Get a cup of herbal tea. Take a nap. Eat lots of fruits & veggies. Hey! it's O.K. to smile, laugh or cry. Jesus loves me; it's time to love me too. Listen to calm classical music, nature sounds, Christian music. Start a garden or get a plant. Adopt a pet. It' alright if I Seek professional help/speak to a trained pastoral counselor at a local church. Who can I help today?

Right Now I Feel:

What Self-Care can help now?

I can forgive myself and:

I am Grateful for:

List Today's Victories:

DATE:

How did I bloom today?

How can I improve?

What did I learn so far?

My Plans for tomorrow with God's help:

Living to Serve:

Who can I help today/tomorrow? Volunteer at:
Soup kitchen   Nursing home   School   Church
Start a group that: Cooks   Sew   Make crafts to share
Collect: food   clothing   books for those in need.
Join a rescue organization to help people or animals
Share Bible studies   Share your journey...

DATE:
TODAY'S TASKS
-
-
-
-
-
-
-
-
-
-

NOW MAY THE GOD OF HOPE FILL YOU WITH ALL JOY AND PEACE IN BELIEVING, SO THAT YOU WILL ABOUND IN HOPE BY THE POWER OF THE HOLY SPIRIT.
ROMANS 15:13
I CAN BLOOM!

Prayer: Lord, I need your strength to get through this day, in Jesus name; Amen.

My Self-Care checklist:

Prayer/Read Bible - Breakfast - Shower - Hair - Dress - Exercise - Lunch - Prayer - Encourage 2 Persons - Local Support Groups - Dinner - Get my at home massage - Take a soothing bath - Get a cup of herbal tea. Take a nap. Eat lots of fruits & veggies. Hey! it's O.K. to smile, laugh or cry. Jesus loves me; it's time to love me too. Listen to calm classical music, nature sounds, Christian music. Start a garden or get a plant. Adopt a pet. It' alright if I Seek professional help/speak to a trained pastoral counselor at a local church. Who can I help today?

Right Now I Feel:
_____
_____

What Self-Care can help now?
_____
_____

I can forgive myself and:
_____
_____

I am Grateful for:
_____
_____
_____

List Today's Victories:
_____
_____
_____

DATE:

How did I bloom today?

How can I improve?

What did I learn so far?

My Plans for tomorrow with God's help:

Living to Serve:

Who can I help today/tomorrow? Volunteer at:
Soup kitchen   Nursing home   School   Church
Start a group that: Cooks   Sew   Make crafts to share
Collect: food   clothing   books for those in need.
Join a rescue organization to help people or animals
Share Bible studies   Share your journey...

DATE:
TODAY'S TASKS

-
-
-
-
-
-
-
-
-

THE LORD YOUR GOD IN YOUR MIDST, THE MIGHTY ONE, WILL SAVE; HE WILL REJOICE OVER YOU WITH GLADNESS, HE WILL QUIET YOU WITH HIS LOVE, HE WILL REJOICE OVER YOU WITH SINGING.
ZEPHANIAH 3:17
I CAN BLOOM!

Prayer: Lord, I need your strength to get through this day, in Jesus name; Amen.

My Self-Care checklist:

Prayer/Read Bible - Breakfast - Shower - Hair - Dress - Exercise - Lunch- Prayer - Encourage 2 Persons - Local Support Groups - Dinner - Get my at home massage - Take a soothing bath - Get a cup of herbal tea. Take a nap. Eat lots of fruits & veggies. Hey! it's O.K. to smile, laugh or cry. Jesus loves me; it's time to love me too. Listen to calm classical music, nature sounds, Christian music. Start a garden or get a plant. Adopt a pet. It' alright if I Seek professional help/speak to a trained pastoral counselor at a local church. Who can I help today?

Right Now I Feel:
_____
_____

What Self-Care can help now?
_____
_____

I can forgive myself and:
_____
_____

I am Grateful for:
_____
_____
_____

List Today's Victories:
_____
_____
_____

DATE:

How did I bloom today?

How can I improve?

What did I learn so far?

My Plans for tomorrow with God's help:

Living to Serve:

Who can I help today/tomorrow? Volunteer at:
Soup kitchen   Nursing home   School   Church
Start a group that: Cooks   Sew   Make crafts to share
Collect: food   clothing   books for those in need.
Join a rescue organization to help people or animals
Share Bible studies   Share your journey…

DATE:
TODAY'S TASKS

-
-
-
-
-
-
-
-
-

EVEN THOUGH I WALK THROUGH THE DARKEST VALLEY, I WILL FEAR NO EVIL, FOR YOU, LORD ARE WITH ME; YOUR ROD AND YOUR STAFF, THEY COMFORT ME. PSALM 23:4
I CAN BLOOM!

Prayer: Lord, I need your strength to get through this day, in Jesus name; Amen.

My Self-Care checklist :

Prayer/Read Bible - Breakfast - Shower - Hair - Dress - Exercise - Lunch - Prayer - Encourage 2 Persons - Local Support Groups - Dinner - Get my at home massage - Take a soothing bath - Get a cup of herbal tea. Take a nap. Eat lots of fruits & veggies. Hey! it's O.K. to smile, laugh or cry. Jesus loves me; it's time to love me too. Listen to calm classical music, nature sounds, Christian music. Start a garden or get a plant. Adopt a pet. It' alright if I Seek professional help/speak to a trained pastoral counselor at a local church. Who can I help today?

Right Now I Feel: _____

What Self-Care can help now? _____

I can forgive myself and: _____

I am Grateful for: _____

List Today's Victories: _____

DATE:

How did I bloom today?

How can I improve?

What did I learn so far?

My Plans for tomorrow with God's help:

Living to Serve:

Who can I help today/tomorrow? Volunteer at:
Soup kitchen   Nursing home   School   Church
Start a group that: Cooks   Sew   Make crafts to share
Collect: food   clothing   books for those in need.
Join a rescue organization to help people or animals
Share Bible studies   Share your journey...

DATE:

"God's promise to all who mourn... is to give you the lasting beauty of His grace and presence instead of the ashes of sorrow; the oil of joy instead of mourning and a garment that desires to praise God instead of a heart burdened with despair... ." Isaiah 61:3.

<u>Part of My Self-Care is to See and Experience Beauty Again.</u>

Father in heaven, please help me to accept and experience the the beauty of Your Grace and Presence; in Jesus name, Amen.

<u>My Thoughts about God's beauty for me:</u>
_____
_____
_____
_____
_____
_____
_____
_____
_____
_____

DATE:

How can I bloom in God's Beauty Today?

What did I learn about God Today?

Write the names of people you can help to see God's beauty in their lives and help them asap.

Living to Serve:

Who can I help today/tomorrow? Volunteer at:
Soup kitchen   Nursing home   School   Church
Start a group that: Cooks   Sew   Make crafts to share
Collect: food   clothing   books for those in need.
Join a rescue organization to help people or animals
Share Bible studies   Share your journey…

DATE:

"God's promise to all who mourn... is to give you the lasting beauty of His grace and presence instead of the ashes of sorrow; the oil of joy instead of mourning and a garment that desires to praise God instead of a heart burdened with despair... ."
Isaiah 61:3.

<u>Part of My Self-Care is to See and Experience Joy Again.</u>

Father in heaven, please help me to accept and experience Your oil of Joy today and always; in Jesus name, Amen.

<u>My Thoughts about God's oil of joy for me:</u> _____
_____
_____
_____
_____
_____
_____
_____
_____
_____

DATE: _____

How can I bloom in God's Oil of Joy Today?

_____
_____
_____
_____
_____

What did I learn about God Today?
_____
_____
_____
_____
_____
_____
_____
_____
_____

Write the names of people you can share God's oil of Joy with and help them asap.
_____
_____
_____
_____
_____
_____

<u>Living to Serve:</u>

Who can I help today/tomorrow? Volunteer at:
Soup kitchen   Nursing home   School   Church
Start a group that: Cooks   Sew   Make crafts to share
Collect: food   clothing   books for those in need.
Join a rescue organization to help people or animals
Share Bible studies   Share your journey…

DATE:

"God's promise to all who mourn... is to give you the lasting beauty of His grace and presence instead of the ashes of sorrow; the oil of joy instead of mourning and a garment that desires to praise God instead of a heart burdened with despair... ."
Isaiah 61:3.

<u>Part of My Self-Care is to Desire to Praise God.</u>

Father in heaven, please create in me the desire to praise You today and always because You deserve the Glory and the Praise for who You are; in Jesus name, Amen.

<u>My Thoughts about God adorning/ clothing my heart in His righteousness with the Desire to Praise Him:</u>

_____
_____
_____
_____
_____
_____
_____
_____
_____
_____

DATE:

How can I bloom in Praise to God Today?

_____
_____
_____
_____
_____

What did I learn about God Today?
_____
_____
_____
_____
_____
_____
_____
_____
_____

Write the names of people who you can share a testimony with about God and His goodness to you; you can share the Bible text in Isaiah 61:3 to help them.
_____
_____
_____
_____
_____

Living to Serve:

Who can I help today/tomorrow? Volunteer at:
Soup kitchen   Nursing home   School   Church
Start a group that: Cooks   Sew   Make crafts to share
Collect: food   clothing   books for those in need.
Join a rescue organization to help people or animals
Share Bible studies   Share your journey…

Father in heaven, thank you for bringing me out of my distress; in Jesus name, Amen.

DATE:

Psalm 107:28-31 Yet when they cried out to the Lord in their trouble, the Lord brought them out of their distress. He calmed the storm and its waves quieted down. So they rejoiced that the waves became quiet, and he led them to their desired haven. Let them give thanks to the Lord for his gracious love and for his awesome deeds on behalf of all humanity.

My Thoughts about God bringing me out of my distress:

_____
_____
_____
_____
_____
_____
_____
_____
_____
_____

DATE:

How can I bloom today to show how God is bringing me out of my distress?

What did I learn about God Today?

What changes can I make in my life as God brings me out of my distress?

Living to Serve:

Who can I help today/tomorrow? Volunteer at:
Soup kitchen   Nursing home   School   Church
Start a group that: Cooks   Sew   Make crafts to share
Collect: food   clothing   books for those in need.
Join a rescue organization to help people or animals
Share Bible studies   Share your journey…

Father in heaven, thank you for Your peace that calms the storm in my life; in Jesus name, Amen.

DATE:

Psalm 107:28-31 Yet when they cried out to the Lord in their trouble, the Lord brought them out of their distress. He calmed the storm and its waves quieted down. So they rejoiced that the waves became quiet, and he led them to their desired haven. Let them give thanks to the Lord for his gracious love and for his awesome deeds on behalf of all humanity.

My Thoughts about God's peace that calms the storm in my life:

_____
_____
_____
_____
_____
_____
_____
_____
_____
_____

DATE:

How can I bloom in God's peace that calms my storm? _____

What did I learn about God Today?
_____
_____
_____
_____
_____
_____
_____
_____

What changes can I make in my life as God gives me peace?
_____
_____
_____
_____
_____

Living to Serve:

Who can I help today/tomorrow? Volunteer at:
Soup kitchen   Nursing home   School   Church
Start a group that: Cooks   Sew   Make crafts to share
Collect: food   clothing   books for those in need.
Join a rescue organization to help people or animals
Share Bible studies   Share your journey…

Father in heaven, I rejoice as You lead me to a place of safety in You; in Jesus name, Amen.

DATE:

Psalm 107:28-31 Yet when they cried out to the Lord in their trouble, the Lord brought them out of their distress. He calmed the storm and its waves quieted down. So they rejoiced that the waves became quiet, and he led them to their desired haven. Let them give thanks to the Lord for his gracious love and for his awesome deeds on behalf of all humanity.

My Thoughts about God leading me to a safe place:

_____
_____
_____
_____
_____
_____
_____
_____
_____

DATE:

How can I bloom today knowing that God is leading me to a safe place?

_____
_____
_____
_____
_____
_____

What did I learn about God Today?

_____
_____
_____
_____
_____
_____
_____
_____

What changes can I make in my life as I trust God to lead me to safety?

_____
_____
_____
_____
_____
_____

Living to Serve:

Who can I help today/tomorrow? Volunteer at:
Soup kitchen   Nursing home   School   Church
Start a group that: Cooks   Sew   Make crafts to share
Collect: food   clothing   books for those in need.
Join a rescue organization to help people or animals
Share Bible studies   Share your journey…

Father in heaven, I am grateful for your gracious love and the great work you do on my behalf; in Jesus name, Amen.

DATE:

Psalm 107:28-31 Yet when they cried out to the Lord in their trouble, the Lord brought them out of their distress. He calmed the storm and its waves quieted down. So they rejoiced that the waves became quiet, and he led them to their desired haven. Let them give thanks to the Lord for his gracious love and for his awesome deeds on behalf of all humanity.

My Thoughts about God's love to me and all He has done and is doing for me:

_____
_____
_____
_____
_____
_____
_____
_____
_____
_____

DATE:

How can I bloom knowing that God loves me and is working on my behalf?

What did I learn about God Today?

What changes can I make in my life because I know God loves me and is working on my behalf?

Living to Serve:

Who can I help today/tomorrow? Volunteer at:
Soup kitchen   Nursing home   School   Church
Start a group that: Cooks   Sew   Make crafts to share
Collect: food   clothing   books for those in need.
Join a rescue organization to help people or animals
Share Bible studies   Share your journey…

DATE:

<u>My Self-Care: Forgiveness</u>

Create a beautiful bouquet of daffodils today. You will need some coloring pencils. These plain designs need your help to make them vibrant and beautiful.

After coloring the flowers, fill out the tag to yourself.

Look around you and find something that you can enhance to make beautiful.

List Today's Victories:

_____
_____
_____
_____

DATE:

My Self-Care: Forgiveness

Create a beautiful bouquet of flowers today. You will need some coloring pencils. These plain designs need your help to make them vibrant and beautiful.

After coloring the flowers, write the name of someone you need to forgive.

Look around you and find something that you can share with someone to help them to have a beautiful day.

List Today's Victories:

DATE: *My Self-Care: Letter Writing*

So, you are missing your loved one. It is alright to acknowledge those feelings. Now, you can write a letter to this person. Just share what's on your heart even though you cannot physically give it to the person.
This will help you on your journey towards healing.

DATE:

My Self-Care: Letter Writing

So, you are missing your loved one. It is alright to acknowledge those feelings. Now, you can write a letter to this person. Just share what's on your heart even though you cannot physically give it to the person.

This will help you on your journey towards healing.

I Miss you

DATE:

How can I honor the memory of my loved one?

Some Suggestions:

Prayer: Lord, I give you the glory for the memories of my loved one. Please guide my choices as I honor their memory, in Jesus name; Amen.

Finish a meaningful project they started
Give to their favorite charity
Start a garden and plant some of their favorites
Eat some of their favorite foods and share with family and friends

Live your life with honor
Learn one of their hobbies
Create a scholarship in their name
Read some of their favorite Bible verses
Share their jokes
Sing some of their favorite songs
Memorial Service

I will

DATE:

How can I honor the memory of my loved one?

Some Suggestions:

Prayer: Lord, I give you the glory for the memories of my loved one. Please guide my choices as I honor their memory, in Jesus name; Amen.

- Finish a meaningful project they started
- Give to their favorite charity
- Start a garden and plant some of their favorites
- Eat some of their favorite foods and share with family and friends
- Live your life with honor
- Learn one of their hobbies
- Create a scholarship in their name
- Read some of their favorite Bible verses
- Share their jokes
- Sing some of their favorite songs
- Memorial Service

I will

DATE:

Make a list of Positive People I can call or Support Groups I can Join

Be careful to choose people who are interested in your well-being and can be a positive influence in your life. The care you receive will help you to share and care for others in their time of need.

2 Corinthians 1:3-4: "Blessed be the God and Father of our Lord Jesus Christ, the Father of mercies and God of all comfort, who comforts us in all our affliction, so that we may be able to comfort those who are in any affliction, with the comfort with which we ourselves are comforted by God."

How can I apply this positive affirmation to my life?
Who else can I affirm today?

DATE:

Make a list of Positive People I can call or Support Groups I can Join

Be careful to choose people who are interested in your well-being and can be a positive influence in your life. The care you receive will help you to share and care for others in their time of need.

2 Corinthians 1:3-4: "Blessed be the God and Father of our Lord Jesus Christ, the Father of mercies and God of all comfort, who comforts us in all our affliction, so that we may be able to comfort those who are in any affliction, with the comfort with which we ourselves are comforted by God."

How can I apply this positive affirmation to my life?
Who else can I affirm today?

DATE:

**JOB 8:21 - HE WILL YET FILL YOUR MOUTH WITH LAUGHTER AND YOUR LIPS WITH SHOUTS OF JOY.
I CAN BLOOM!**

My Self-Care of Laughter:

Prayer: Father in heaven I need your gift of laughter to decrease my stress and improve my mental and physical health, in Jesus name; Amen.

Funny moments:

How do you feel after laughing?
_____
_____
_____
_____
_____

Recall some of your own funny moments:
_____
_____
_____
_____
_____
_____

DATE:

My Self-Care of Laughter:

**JOB 8:21 - HE WILL YET FILL YOUR MOUTH WITH LAUGHTER AND YOUR LIPS WITH SHOUTS OF JOY.
I CAN BLOOM!**

Prayer: Father in heaven I need your gift of laughter to decrease my stress and improve my mental and physical health, in Jesus name; Amen.

Funny moments:

How do you feel after laughing?
_____
_____
_____
_____
_____

Recall some of your own funny moments:
_____
_____
_____
_____
_____

DATE:

JOB 8:21 - HE WILL YET FILL YOUR MOUTH WITH LAUGHTER AND YOUR LIPS WITH SHOUTS OF JOY. I CAN BLOOM!

Prayer: Father in heaven I need your gift of laughter to decrease my stress and improve my mental and physical health, in Jesus name; Amen.

My Self-Care of Laughter :

Funny moments:

How do you feel after laughing?
_____
_____
_____
_____
_____
_____

Recall some of your own funny moments:
_____
_____
_____
_____
_____
_____
_____

DATE:

**JOB 8:21 - HE WILL YET FILL YOUR MOUTH WITH LAUGHTER AND YOUR LIPS WITH SHOUTS OF JOY.
I CAN BLOOM!**

Prayer: Father in heaven I need your gift of laughter to decrease my stress and improve my mental and physical health, in Jesus name; Amen.

My Self-Care of Laughter:

Funny moments:

How do you feel after laughing?
_____
_____
_____
_____
_____
_____
_____

Recall some of your own funny moments:
_____
_____
_____
_____
_____
_____
_____

Holidays / Special Days

**MY PLANS TO COPE DURING THE HOLIDAY/SPECIAL DAY.
I CAN BLOOM!**

I will bravely accept other people's memories of my loved one and I will share my own.

Prayer: Lord, I need your strength to get through this special day, in Jesus name; Amen.

What Self-Care can help now?

Today is:

I feel:

I can share favorite foods, pictures, conversations, games etc. Make a list:

I am Grateful for:

List Today's Victories:

Holidays / Special Days

**MY PLANS TO COPE DURING THE HOLIDAY/SPECIAL DAY.
I CAN BLOOM!**

I will bravely accept other people's memories of my loved one and I will share my own. What Self-Care can help now?

Prayer: Lord, I need your strength to get through this special day, in Jesus name; Amen.

Today is:

I feel:

I can share favorite foods, pictures, conversations, games etc. Make a list:

I am Grateful for:

List Today's Victories:

Holidays / Special Days

MY PLANS TO COPE DURING THE HOLIDAY/SPECIAL DAY.
I CAN BLOOM!

I will bravely accept other people's memories of my loved one and I will share my own.

Prayer: Lord, I need your strength to get through this special day, in Jesus name; Amen.

What Self-Care can help now?

Today is:

I feel:

I can share favorite foods, pictures, conversations, games etc. Make a list:

I am Grateful for:

List Today's Victories:

Holidays / Special Days

MY PLANS TO COPE DURING THE HOLIDAY/SPECIAL DAY.
I CAN BLOOM!

I will bravely accept other people's memories of my loved one and I will share my own.

What Self-Care can help now?

Today is:

I feel:

I can share favorite foods, pictures, conversations, games etc. Make a list:

Prayer: Lord, I need your strength to get through this special day, in Jesus name; Amen.

I am Grateful for:

List Today's Victories:

Holidays / Special Days

MY PLANS TO COPE DURING THE HOLIDAY/SPECIAL DAY.
I CAN BLOOM!

I will bravely accept other people's memories of my loved one and I will share my own. What Self-Care can help now?

Prayer: Lord, I need your strength to get through this special day, in Jesus name; Amen.

Today is:

I feel:

I can share favorite foods, pictures, conversations, games etc. Make a list:

I am Grateful for:

List Today's Victories:

Holidays / Special Days

MY PLANS TO COPE DURING THE HOLIDAY/SPECIAL DAY.
I CAN BLOOM!

I will bravely accept other people's memories of my loved one and I will share my own.

Prayer: Lord, I need your strength to get through this special day, in Jesus name; Amen.

What Self-Care can help now?

Today is:

I feel:

I can share favorite foods, pictures, conversations, games etc. Make a list:

I am Grateful for:

List Today's Victories:

DATE:
TODAY'S TASKS

-
-
-
-
-
-
-
-
-

**My Self-Care:
Write a Letter to Yourself**

Prayer: Father in heaven, Please help me to look at myself honestly and be kind despite my imperfections; in Jesus name, Amen.

Example: an apology, forgiveness, making peace with self, promise to take better care, promise to speak positive words etc.

Dear _____

DATE:

**THE LORD IS MY SHEPHERD; I SHALL NOT WANT. HE MAKES ME TO LIE DOWN IN GREEN PASTURES: HE LEADS ME BESIDE THE STILL WATERS. HE RESTORES MY SOUL: HE LEADS ME IN THE PATHS OF RIGHTEOUSNESS FOR HIS NAME'S SAKE.
PSALM 23:1-3
I CAN BLOOM!**

Add a New Picture of Yourself

Positive Self-Reflection: Look at yourself and share Only positive words.

This Moment Alone with Me Feels:

When I look at myself, I see

With God as my Shepherd, I can begin again. I can make some positive changes such as:

DATE:
TODAY'S TASKS
-
-
-
-
-
-
-
-
-

**My Self-Care:
Write a Letter to Yourself**

Prayer: Father in heaven, Please help me to look at myself honestly and be kind despite my imperfections; in Jesus name, Amen.

Example: an apology, forgiveness, making peace with self, promise to take better care, promise to speak positive words etc.

Dear _____

DATE:

THE LORD IS MY SHEPHERD; I SHALL NOT WANT. HE MAKES ME TO LIE DOWN IN GREEN PASTURES: HE LEADS ME BESIDE THE STILL WATERS. HE RESTORES MY SOUL: HE LEADS ME IN THE PATHS OF RIGHTEOUSNESS FOR HIS NAME'S SAKE. PSALM 23:1-3
I CAN BLOOM!

Add a New Picture of Yourself

Positive Self-Reflection: Look at yourself and share Only positive words.

This Moment Alone with Me Feels:

When I look at myself, I see

With God as my Shepherd, I can begin again. I can make some positive changes such as:

DATE:

TODAY'S TASKS

-
-
-
-
-
-
-
-
-

**My Self-Care:
Write a Letter to family/friend**

Prayer: Father in heaven, Please help me to look at others honestly and be kind despite their imperfections; in Jesus name, Amen.

Example: an apology, forgiveness, making peace with person, promise to take better care, promise to speak positive words etc.

Dear _____

DATE:

THE LORD IS MY SHEPHERD; I SHALL NOT WANT. HE MAKES ME TO LIE DOWN IN GREEN PASTURES: HE LEADS ME BESIDE THE STILL WATERS. HE RESTORES MY SOUL: HE LEADS ME IN THE PATHS OF RIGHTEOUSNESS FOR HIS NAME'S SAKE. PSALM 23:1-3
I CAN BLOOM!

Add a Picture of family/friends

Positive Self-Reflection: Look at others and share Only positive words.

This Moment Alone with Me or with family/friend Feels:

When I look at family/friend I see

With God as my Shepherd, I can begin again. I can make some positive changes such as:

DATE:
TODAY'S TASKS

-
-
-
-
-
-
-
-
-

John 3:16

My Self-Care:
Write a Letter to Jesus

Prayer: Father in heaven, Please help me to look at You as a loving God who only wants the very best for me; in Jesus name, Amen.

Example: an apology, asking God's forgiveness, making peace with God, desire to study the Bible and spend more time talking and listening to God daily.

Dear _____

_____
_____
_____
_____
_____
_____
_____
_____
_____
_____
_____
_____
_____
_____

DATE:

TODAY'S TASKS

-
-
-
-
-
-
-
-
-

John 3:16

My Self-Care:
Write a Letter to Jesus

Prayer: Father in heaven, Please help me to look at You as a loving God who only wants the very best for me; in Jesus name, Amen.

Example: an apology, asking God's forgiveness, making peace with God, desire to study the Bible and spend more time talking and listening to God daily.

Dear _____

DATE:
TODAY'S TASKS
-
-
-
-
-
-
-
-
-
-

FOR GOD SO LOVED THE WORLD THAT HE GAVE HIS ONLY SON THAT WHOEVER BELIEVES IN JESUS WILL NOT PERISH, BUT WILL HAVE ETERNAL LIFE. JOHN 3:16.
I CAN BLOOM!

Prayer: Father in heaven, Please send your Holy Spirit to guide me into the truth about Your love for me and others, in Jesus name; Amen.

My Self-Care Spirituality:

God, I thank you for loving me and in response to your love, I will:

1.

2.

3.

4.

Who can I share this news with?

DATE:

What will I do with God's gift of Eternal Life?

What did I learn so far?

_____
_____
_____
_____
_____
_____
_____
_____

My Plans for tomorrow with God's help:

_____
_____
_____
_____

Living to Serve:

Who can I help today/tomorrow? Volunteer at:
Soup kitchen   Nursing home   School   Church
Start a group that: Cooks   Sew   Make crafts to share
Collect: food   clothing   books for those in need.
Join a rescue organization to help people or animals
Share Bible studies   Share your journey…

DATE:
TODAY'S TASKS
-
-
-
-
-
-
-
-
-

IF WE CONFESS OUR SINS, HE IS FAITHFUL AND JUST AND WILL FORGIVE US OUR SINS AND PURIFY US FROM ALL UNRIGHTEOUSNESS .1 JOHN 1:19.
I CAN BLOOM!

Prayer: Father in heaven, Please send your Holy Spirit to guide me into the truth about Your love for me and others, in Jesus name; Amen.

My Self-Care Spirituality :

God, I thank you for forgivng me and for purifying my heart from All sins. I am listing personal attitudes that I need you to help me to overcome:

1.

2.

3.

4.

Write a simple prayer.

DATE:
TODAY'S TASKS
-
-
-
-
-
-
-
-
-

IF WE CONFESS OUR SINS, HE IS FAITHFUL AND JUST AND WILL FORGIVE US OUR SINS AND PURIFY US FROM ALL UNRIGHTEOUSNESS .1 JOHN 1:19.
I CAN BLOOM!

Prayer: Father in heaven, Please send your Holy Spirit to guide me into the truth about Your love for me and others, in Jesus name; Amen.

My Self-Care Spirituality:

God, I thank you for forgivng me and for purifying my heart from All sins. I am listing the names of each person that I am asking You to save:

1.

2.

3.

4.

Who else can I pray for?

DATE:

How can I share the love of Jesus?

I can gift Journals to a grieving person or group and work with them.

My Plans to help others who are grieving:

Living to Serve:

Who can I help today/tomorrow? Volunteer at:
Soup kitchen   Nursing home   School   Church
Start a group that: Cooks   Sew   Make crafts to share
Collect: food   clothing   books for those in need.
Join a rescue organization to help people or animals
Share Bible studies   Share your journey…

DATE:

How can I share the love of Jesus?

I can gift Journals to a grieving person or group and work with them.

My Plans to help others who are grieving:

Living to Serve:

Who can I help today/tomorrow? Volunteer at:
Soup kitchen   Nursing home   School   Church
Start a group that: Cooks   Sew   Make crafts to share
Collect: food   clothing   books for those in need.
Join a rescue organization to help people or animals
Share Bible studies   Share your journey...

DATE:
TODAY'S TASKS

-
-
-
-
-
-
-
-
-

GOD, SURELY, YOUR GOODNESS AND LOVE WILL FOLLOW ME ALL THE DAYS OF MY LIFE AND I WILL DWELL IN THE HOUSE OF THE LORD FOREVER.
PSALM 23:6

I CAN BLOOM!

How do you feel knowing that God is following you to do good to you?

_____
_____
_____
_____

What will you do differently today?

_____
_____

I am Grateful for:

_____
_____
_____

List Today's Victories:

_____
_____
_____

DATE:

How did I bloom today? _____

How can I improve? _____

Who can I serve today to share God's goodness?
_____
_____
_____
_____
_____
_____
_____
_____

My Plans for tomorrow with God's help:
_____
_____
_____
_____
_____

Living to Serve:

Who can I help today/tomorrow? Volunteer at:
Soup kitchen   Nursing home   School   Church
Start a group that: Cooks   Sew   Make crafts to share
Collect: food   clothing   books for those in need.
Join a rescue organization to help people or animals
Share Bible studies   Share your journey...

DATE:
TODAY'S TASKS
-
-
-
-
-
-
-
-
-

GOD, SURELY, YOUR GOODNESS AND LOVE WILL FOLLOW ME ALL THE DAYS OF MY LIFE AND I WILL DWELL IN THE HOUSE OF THE LORD FOREVER.
PSALM 23:6
I CAN BLOOM!

How do I Feel about My Progress so far?
_____
_____
_____
_____
_____
_____
_____

I am Grateful for:
_____
_____
_____

How many tasks did I accomplish today?
_____
_____
_____
_____

DATE:

How did I bloom today?

_____
_____
_____
_____
_____

List 2-5 Victories I had on this Journey:

_____
_____
_____
_____
_____
_____
_____
_____

My Plans for tomorrow with God's help:

_____
_____
_____
_____
_____
_____

Living to Serve:

Who can I help today/tomorrow? Volunteer at:
Soup kitchen   Nursing home   School   Church
Start a group that: Cooks   Sew   Make crafts to share
Collect: food   clothing   books for those in need.
Join a rescue organization to help people or animals
Share Bible studies   Share your journey…

Congratulations!

You are on a New Journey Now!
It's time to reflect on all that you learned and implemented
from the Grief Course and the Grief Journal.
Use what you learned to write new goals for your life.
Feel free to revisit the sections of the course and journal.
Share your testimony so others can learn from you.

Father in heaven, thank you for leading me through this process. I am
trusting You with all my goals for the future.
I know that in All these
things I am more than conqueror through Jesus who loves me. Amen.
Romans 8:37.

Out of My Grief I Bloom!

Goal # :

Steps to Accomplish My Goal:

Congratulations!

You are on a New Journey Now!
It's time to reflect on all that you learned and implemented
from the Grief Course and the Grief Journal.
Use what you learned to write new goals for your life.
Feel free to revisit the sections of the course and journal.
Share your testimony so others can learn from you.

Father in heaven, thank you for leading me through this process. I am
trusting You with all my goals for the future.
I know that in All these
things I am more than conqueror through Jesus who loves me. Amen.
Romans 8:37.

Out of My Grief I Bloom!

Goal # :

Steps to Accomplish My Goal:

Congratulations!

You are on a New Journey Now!
It's time to reflect on all that you learned and implemented
from the Grief Course and the Grief Journal.
Use what you learned to write new goals for your life.
Feel free to revisit the sections of the course and journal.
Share your testimony so others can learn from you.

Father in heaven, thank you for leading me through this process. I am
trusting You with all my goals for the future.
I know that in All these
things I am more than conqueror through Jesus who loves me. Amen.
Romans 8:37.

Out of My Grief I Bloom!

Goal # :

Steps to Accomplish My Goal:

Congratulations!

You are on a New Journey Now!
It's time to reflect on all that you learned and implemented
from the Grief Course and the Grief Journal.
Use what you learned to write new goals for your life.
Feel free to revisit the sections of the course and journal.
Share your testimony so others can learn from you.

Father in heaven, thank you for leading me through this process. I am
trusting You with all my goals for the future.
I know that in All these
things I am more than conqueror through Jesus who loves me. Amen.
Romans 8:37.

Out of My Grief I Bloom!

Goal # :

Steps to Accomplish My Goal:

Congratulations!

You are on a New Journey Now!
It's time to reflect on all that you learned and implemented
from the Grief Course and the Grief Journal.
Use what you learned to write new goals for your life.
Feel free to revisit the sections of the course and journal.
Share your testimony so others can learn from you.

Father in heaven, thank you for leading me through this process. I am trusting You with all my goals for the future.
I know that in All these
things I am more than conqueror through Jesus who loves me. Amen.
Romans 8:37.

Out of My Grief I Bloom!

Goal # :

Steps to Accomplish My Goal:

Congratulations!

You are on a New Journey Now!
It's time to reflect on all that you learned and implemented
from the Grief Course and the Grief Journal.
Use what you learned to write new goals for your life.
Feel free to revisit the sections of the course and journal.
Share your testimony so others can learn from you.

Father in heaven, thank you for leading me through this process. I am
trusting You with all my goals for the future.
I know that in All these
things I am more than conqueror through Jesus who loves me. Amen.
Romans 8:37.

Out of My Grief I Bloom!

Goal # :

Steps to Accomplish My Goal:

Congratulations!

You are on a New Journey Now!
It's time to reflect on all that you learned and implemented
from the Grief Course and the Grief Journal.
Use what you learned to write new goals for your life.
Feel free to revisit the sections of the course and journal.
Share your testimony so others can learn from you.

Father in heaven, thank you for leading me through this process. I am
trusting You with all my goals for the future.
I know that in All these
things I am more than conqueror through Jesus who loves me. Amen.
Romans 8:37.

Out of My Grief I Bloom!

Goal # :

Steps to Accomplish My Goal:

Congratulations!

You are on a New Journey Now!
It's time to reflect on all that you learned and implemented
from the Grief Course and the Grief Journal.
Use what you learned to write new goals for your life.
Feel free to revisit the sections of the course and journal.
Share your testimony so others can learn from you.

Father in heaven, thank you for leading me through this process. I am
trusting You with all my goals for the future.
I know that in All these
things I am more than conqueror through Jesus who loves me. Amen.
Romans 8:37.

Out of My Grief I Bloom!

Goal # :

_____
_____
_____

Steps to Accomplish My Goal:

_____
_____
_____
_____
_____
_____
_____
_____

Congratulations!

You are on a New Journey Now!
It's time to reflect on all that you learned and implemented
from the Grief Course and the Grief Journal.
Use what you learned to write new goals for your life.
Feel free to revisit the sections of the course and journal.
Share your testimony so others can learn from you.

Father in heaven, thank you for leading me through this process. I am
trusting You with all my goals for the future.
I know that in All these
things I am more than conqueror through Jesus who loves me. Amen.
Romans 8:37.

Out of My Grief I Bloom!

Goal # :

Steps to Accomplish My Goal:

Congratulations!

You are on a New Journey Now!
It's time to reflect on all that you learned and implemented
from the Grief Course and the Grief Journal.
Use what you learned to write new goals for your life.
Feel free to revisit the sections of the course and journal.
Share your testimony so others can learn from you.

Father in heaven, thank you for leading me through this process. I am
trusting You with all my goals for the future.
I know that in All these
things I am more than conqueror through Jesus who loves me. Amen.
Romans 8:37.

Out of My Grief I Bloom!

Goal # :

Steps to Accomplish My Goal:

Congratulations!

You are on a New Journey Now!
It's time to reflect on all that you learned and implemented
from the Grief Course and the Grief Journal.
Use what you learned to write new goals for your life.
Feel free to revisit the sections of the course and journal.
Share your testimony so others can learn from you.

Father in heaven, thank you for leading me through this process. I am
trusting You with all my goals for the future.
I know that in All these
things I am more than conqueror through Jesus who loves me. Amen.
Romans 8:37.

Out of My Grief I Bloom!

Goal # :

Steps to Accomplish My Goal:

Congratulations!

You are on a New Journey Now!
It's time to reflect on all that you learned and implemented
from the Grief Course and the Grief Journal.
Use what you learned to write new goals for your life.
Feel free to revisit the sections of the course and journal.
Share your testimony so others can learn from you.

Father in heaven, thank you for leading me through this process. I am trusting You with all my goals for the future.
I know that in All these
things I am more than conqueror through Jesus who loves me. Amen.
Romans 8:37.

Out of My Grief I Bloom!

Goal # :

Steps to Accomplish My Goal:

Congratulations!

You are on a New Journey Now!
It's time to reflect on all that you learned and implemented
from the Grief Course and the Grief Journal.
Use what you learned to write new goals for your life.
Feel free to revisit the sections of the course and journal.
Share your testimony so others can learn from you.

Father in heaven, thank you for leading me through this process. I am
trusting You with all my goals for the future.
I know that in All these
things I am more than conqueror through Jesus who loves me. Amen.
Romans 8:37.

Out of My Grief I Bloom!

Goal # :

Steps to Accomplish My Goal:

Congratulations!

You are on a New Journey Now!
It's time to reflect on all that you learned and implemented
from the Grief Course and the Grief Journal.
Use what you learned to write new goals for your life.
Feel free to revisit the sections of the course and journal.
Share your testimony so others can learn from you.

Father in heaven, thank you for leading me through this process. I am trusting You with all my goals for the future.
I know that in All these
things I am more than conqueror through Jesus who loves me. Amen.
Romans 8:37.

Out of My Grief I Bloom!

Goal # :

Steps to Accomplish My Goal:

Congratulations!

You are on a New Journey Now!
It's time to reflect on all that you learned and implemented
from the Grief Course and the Grief Journal.
Use what you learned to write new goals for your life.
Feel free to revisit the sections of the course and journal.
Share your testimony so others can learn from you.

Father in heaven, thank you for leading me through this process. I am
trusting You with all my goals for the future.
I know that in All these
things I am more than conqueror through Jesus who loves me. Amen.
Romans 8:37.

Out of My Grief I Bloom!

Goal # :

Steps to Accomplish My Goal:

Congratulations!

You are on a New Journey Now!
It's time to reflect on all that you learned and implemented
from the Grief Course and the Grief Journal.
Use what you learned to write new goals for your life.
Feel free to revisit the sections of the course and journal.
Share your testimony so others can learn from you.

Father in heaven, thank you for leading me through this process. I am
trusting You with all my goals for the future.
I know that in All these
things I am more than conqueror through Jesus who loves me. Amen.
Romans 8:37.

Out of My Grief I Bloom!

Goal # :

Steps to Accomplish My Goal:

Congratulations!

You are on a New Journey Now!
It's time to reflect on all that you learned and implemented
from the Grief Course and the Grief Journal.
Use what you learned to write new goals for your life.
Feel free to revisit the sections of the course and journal.
Share your testimony so others can learn from you.

Father in heaven, thank you for leading me through this process. I am
trusting You with all my goals for the future.
I know that in All these
things I am more than conqueror through Jesus who loves me. Amen.
Romans 8:37.

Out of My Grief I Bloom!

Goal # :

Steps to Accomplish My Goal:

Congratulations!

You are on a New Journey Now!
It's time to reflect on all that you learned and implemented from the Grief Course and the Grief Journal.
Use what you learned to write new goals for your life.
Feel free to revisit the sections of the course and journal.
Share your testimony so others can learn from you.

Father in heaven, thank you for leading me through this process. I am trusting You with all my goals for the future.
I know that in All these
things I am more than conqueror through Jesus who loves me. Amen.
Romans 8:37.

Out of My Grief I Bloom!

Goal # :

Steps to Accomplish My Goal:

Congratulations!

You are on a New Journey Now!
It's time to reflect on all that you learned and implemented
from the Grief Course and the Grief Journal.
Use what you learned to write new goals for your life.
Feel free to revisit the sections of the course and journal.
Share your testimony so others can learn from you.

Father in heaven, thank you for leading me through this process. I am
trusting You with all my goals for the future.
I know that in All these
things I am more than conqueror through Jesus who loves me. Amen.
Romans 8:37.

Out of My Grief I Bloom!

Goal # :

Steps to Accomplish My Goal:

Congratulations!

You are on a New Journey Now!
It's time to reflect on all that you learned and implemented
from the Grief Course and the Grief Journal.
Use what you learned to write new goals for your life.
Feel free to revisit the sections of the course and journal.
Share your testimony so others can learn from you.

Father in heaven, thank you for leading me through this process. I am
trusting You with all my goals for the future.
I know that in All these
things I am more than conqueror through Jesus who loves me. Amen.
Romans 8:37.

Out of My Grief I Bloom!

Goal # :

Steps to Accomplish My Goal:

Congratulations!

You are on a New Journey Now!
It's time to reflect on all that you learned and implemented
from the Grief Course and the Grief Journal.
Use what you learned to write new goals for your life.
Feel free to revisit the sections of the course and journal.
Share your testimony so others can learn from you.

Father in heaven, thank you for leading me through this process. I am
trusting You with all my goals for the future.
I know that in All these
things I am more than conqueror through Jesus who loves me. Amen.
Romans 8:37.

Out of My Grief I Bloom!

Goal # :

Steps to Accomplish My Goal:

Congratulations!

You are on a New Journey Now!
It's time to reflect on all that you learned and implemented
from the Grief Course and the Grief Journal.
Use what you learned to write new goals for your life.
Feel free to revisit the sections of the course and journal.
Share your testimony so others can learn from you.

Father in heaven, thank you for leading me through this process. I am trusting You with all my goals for the future.
I know that in All these
things I am more than conqueror through Jesus who loves me. Amen.
Romans 8:37.

Out of My Grief I Bloom!

Goal # :

Steps to Accomplish My Goal:

Congratulations!

You are on a New Journey Now!
It's time to reflect on all that you learned and implemented
from the Grief Course and the Grief Journal.
Use what you learned to write new goals for your life.
Feel free to revisit the sections of the course and journal.
Share your testimony so others can learn from you.

Father in heaven, thank you for leading me through this process. I am
trusting You with all my goals for the future.
I know that in All these
things I am more than conqueror through Jesus who loves me. Amen.
Romans 8:37.

Out of My Grief I Bloom!

Goal # :

Steps to Accomplish My Goal:

Congratulations!

You are on a New Journey Now!
It's time to reflect on all that you learned and implemented
from the Grief Course and the Grief Journal.
Use what you learned to write new goals for your life.
Feel free to revisit the sections of the course and journal.
Share your testimony so others can learn from you.

Father in heaven, thank you for leading me through this process. I am trusting You with all my goals for the future.
I know that in All these
things I am more than conqueror through Jesus who loves me. Amen.
Romans 8:37.

Out of My Grief I Bloom!

Goal # :

Steps to Accomplish My Goal:

Congratulations!

You are on a New Journey Now!
It's time to reflect on all that you learned and implemented
from the Grief Course and the Grief Journal.
Use what you learned to write new goals for your life.
Feel free to revisit the sections of the course and journal.
Share your testimony so others can learn from you.

Father in heaven, thank you for leading me through this process. I am
trusting You with all my goals for the future.
I know that in All these
things I am more than conqueror through Jesus who loves me. Amen.
Romans 8:37.

Out of My Grief I Bloom!

Goal # :

Steps to Accomplish My Goal:

Congratulations!

You are on a New Journey Now!
It's time to reflect on all that you learned and implemented
from the Grief Course and the Grief Journal.
Use what you learned to write new goals for your life.
Feel free to revisit the sections of the course and journal.
Share your testimony so others can learn from you.

Father in heaven, thank you for leading me through this process. I am
trusting You with all my goals for the future.
I know that in All these
things I am more than conqueror through Jesus who loves me. Amen.
Romans 8:37.

Out of My Grief I Bloom!

Goal # :

Steps to Accomplish My Goal:

Congratulations!

You are on a New Journey Now!
It's time to reflect on all that you learned and implemented
from the Grief Course and the Grief Journal.
Use what you learned to write new goals for your life.
Feel free to revisit the sections of the course and journal.
Share your testimony so others can learn from you.

Father in heaven, thank you for leading me through this process. I am
trusting You with all my goals for the future.
I know that in All these
things I am more than conqueror through Jesus who loves me. Amen.
Romans 8:37.

Out of My Grief I Bloom!

Goal # :

Steps to Accomplish My Goal:

Congratulations!

You are on a New Journey Now!
It's time to reflect on all that you learned and implemented
from the Grief Course and the Grief Journal.
Use what you learned to write new goals for your life.
Feel free to revisit the sections of the course and journal.
Share your testimony so others can learn from you.

Father in heaven, thank you for leading me through this process. I am trusting You with all my goals for the future.
I know that in All these
things I am more than conqueror through Jesus who loves me. Amen.
Romans 8:37.

Out of My Grief I Bloom!

Goal # :

Steps to Accomplish My Goal:

Congratulations!

You are on a New Journey Now!
It's time to reflect on all that you learned and implemented
from the Grief Course and the Grief Journal.
Use what you learned to write new goals for your life.
Feel free to revisit the sections of the course and journal.
Share your testimony so others can learn from you.

Father in heaven, thank you for leading me through this process. I am
trusting You with all my goals for the future.
I know that in All these
things I am more than conqueror through Jesus who loves me. Amen.
Romans 8:37.

Out of My Grief I Bloom!

Goal # :

Steps to Accomplish My Goal:

Congratulations!

You are on a New Journey Now!
It's time to reflect on all that you learned and implemented
from the Grief Course and the Grief Journal.
Use what you learned to write new goals for your life.
Feel free to revisit the sections of the course and journal.
Share your testimony so others can learn from you.

Father in heaven, thank you for leading me through this process. I am
trusting You with all my goals for the future.
I know that in All these
things I am more than conqueror through Jesus who loves me. Amen.
Romans 8:37.

Out of My Grief I Bloom!

Goal # :

Steps to Accomplish My Goal:

Helpful Bible Texts:

Philippians 4:13- "I can do all this through him who gives me strength."

Revelation 21:4- "He will wipe every tear from their eyes. There will be no more death or mourning or crying or pain, for the old order of things has passed away."

Psalm 34:18- "The LORD is close to the brokenhearted and saves those who are crushed in spirit."

Romans 8:18- "I consider that our present sufferings are not worth comparing with the glory that will be revealed in us."

Romans 12:2- "Do not conform to the pattern of this world, but be transformed by the renewing of your mind. Then you will be able to test and approve what God's will is—his good, pleasing and perfect will."

Matthew 11:28-30- "Come to me, all you who are weary and burdened, and I will give you rest. Take my yoke upon you and learn from me, for I am gentle and humble in heart, and you will find rest for your souls. For my yoke is easy and my burden is light."

Psalm 147:3- "He heals the brokenhearted and binds up their wounds."

Psalm 23:26- "My flesh and my heart may fail, but God is the strength of my heart and my portion forever."

Matthew 5:4- "Blessed are those who mourn, for they will be comforted."

Joshua 1:9- "Have I not commanded you? Be strong and courageous. Do not be afraid; do not be discouraged, for the LORD your God will be with you wherever you go."

1 Thessalonians 4:13-18- "Brothers and sisters, we do not want you to be uninformed about those who sleep in death so that you do not grieve like the rest of mankind, who have no hope. 14 For we believe that Jesus died and rose again, and so we believe that Jesus will come again and will take those who have fallen asleep in Him.
15 According to the Lord's word, we tell you that we who are still alive until the coming of Jesus, will certainly not precede those who have fallen asleep in death.
16 For the Lord Himself will come down from heaven, with a loud command, with the voice of the archangel and with the trumpet call of God, and the dead in Christ will rise from the grave first.
17 After that, we who are still alive will be caught up together with them in the clouds to meet the Lord in the air. And so, we will be with the Lord forever.
18 Therefore encourage one another with these words."

AMEN